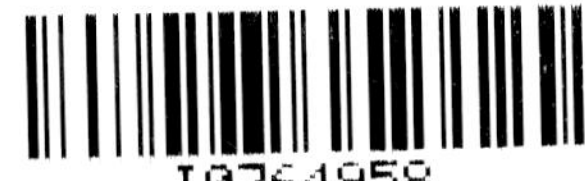

This Elephant Coloring Book Belongs To:

____

____

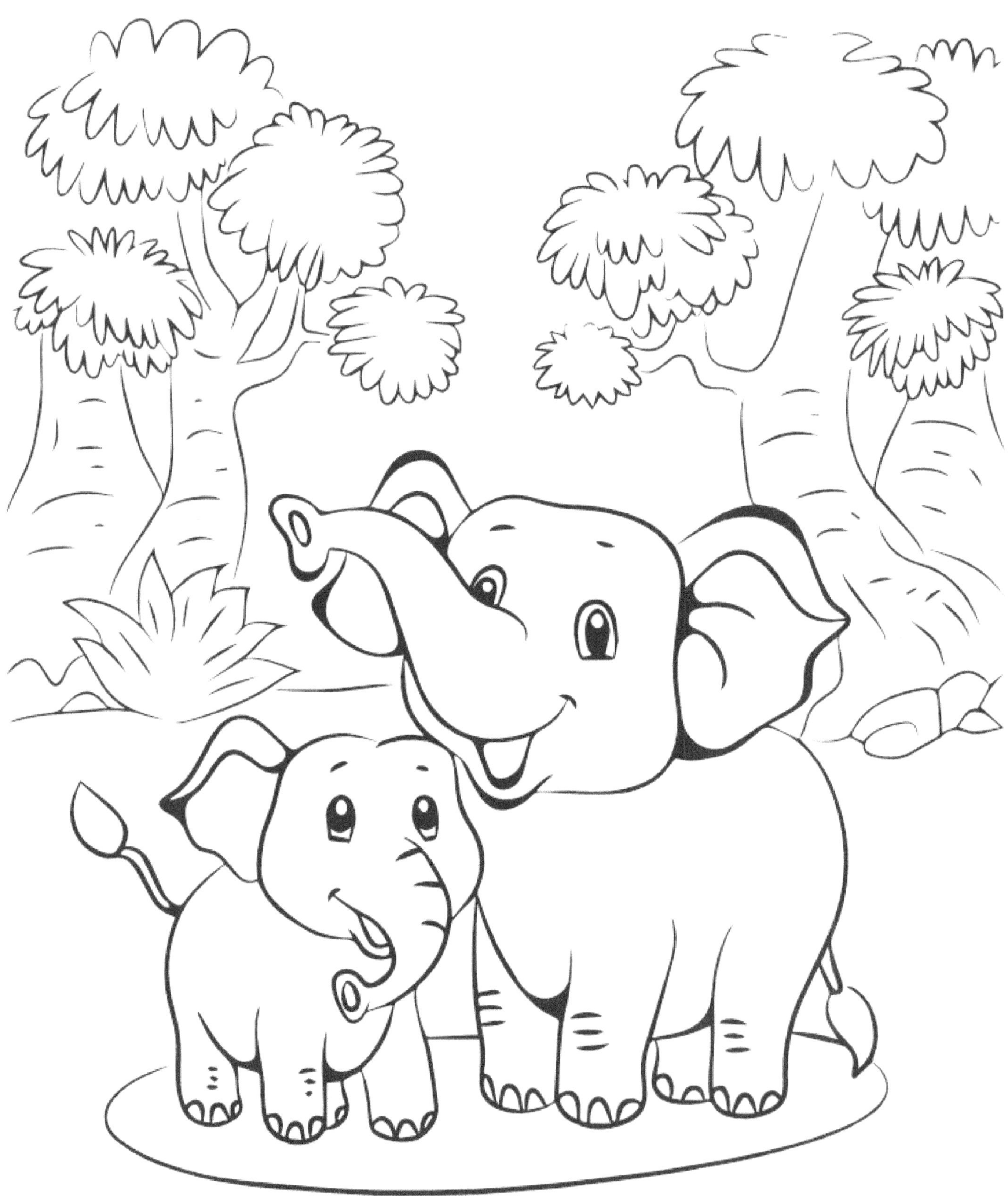

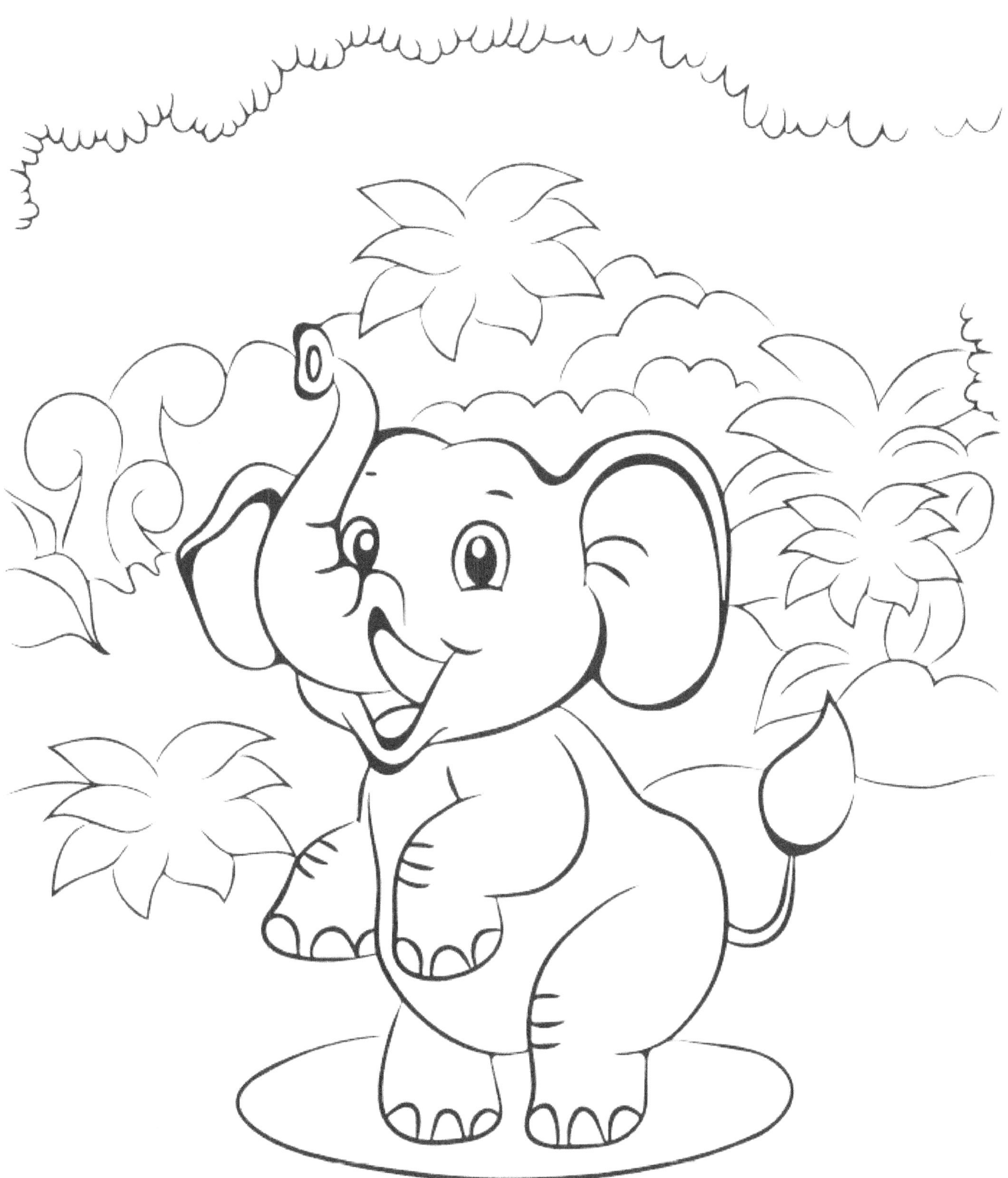

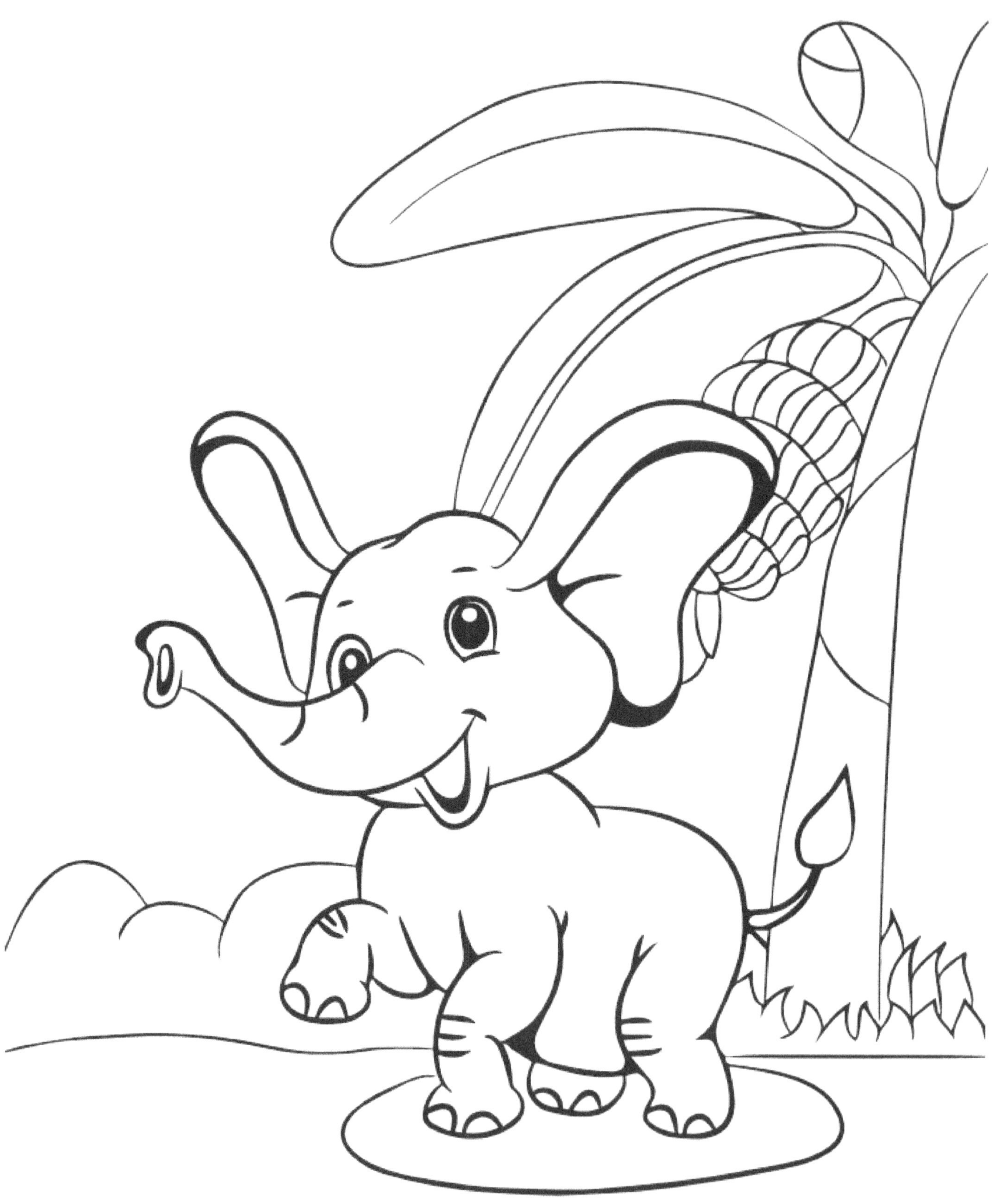

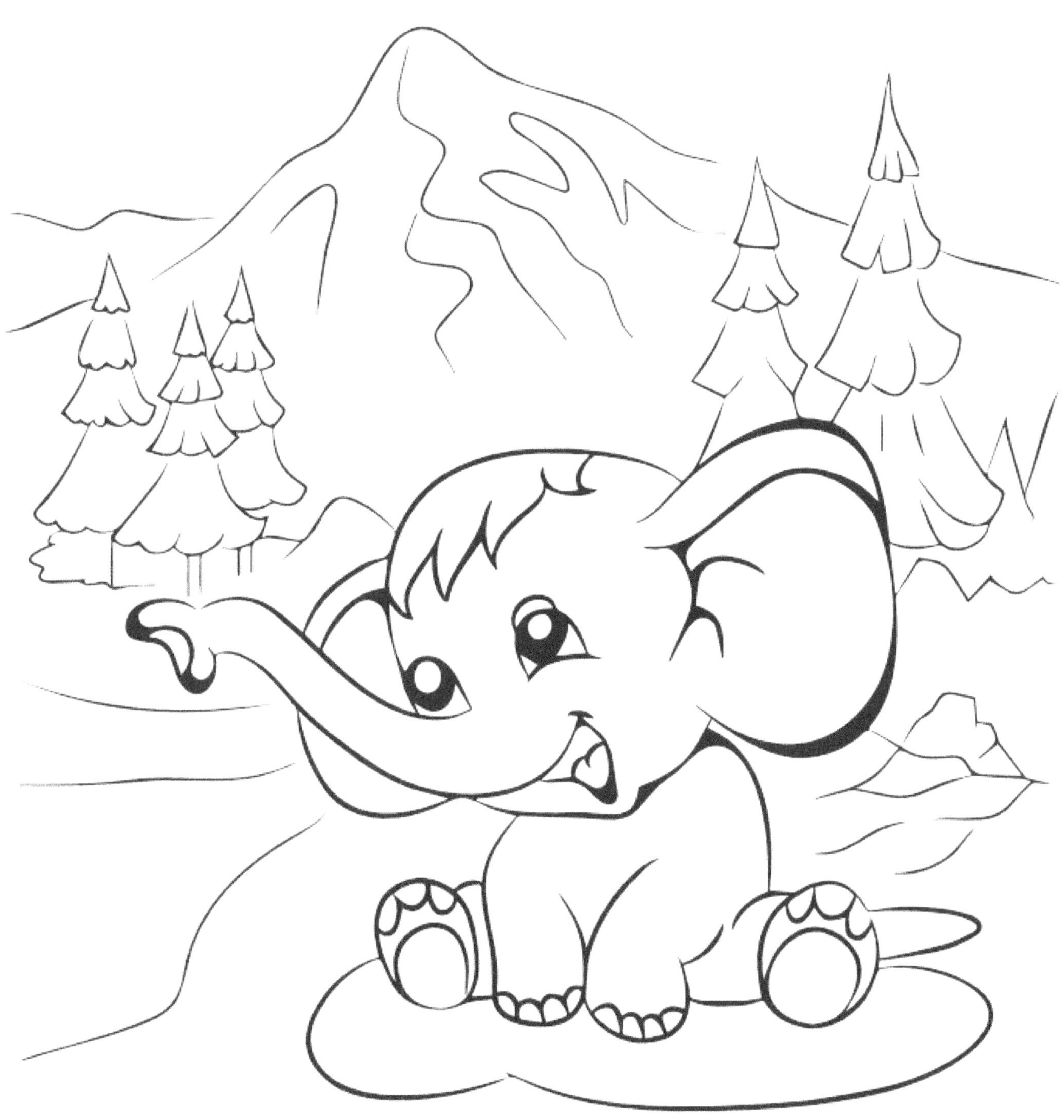

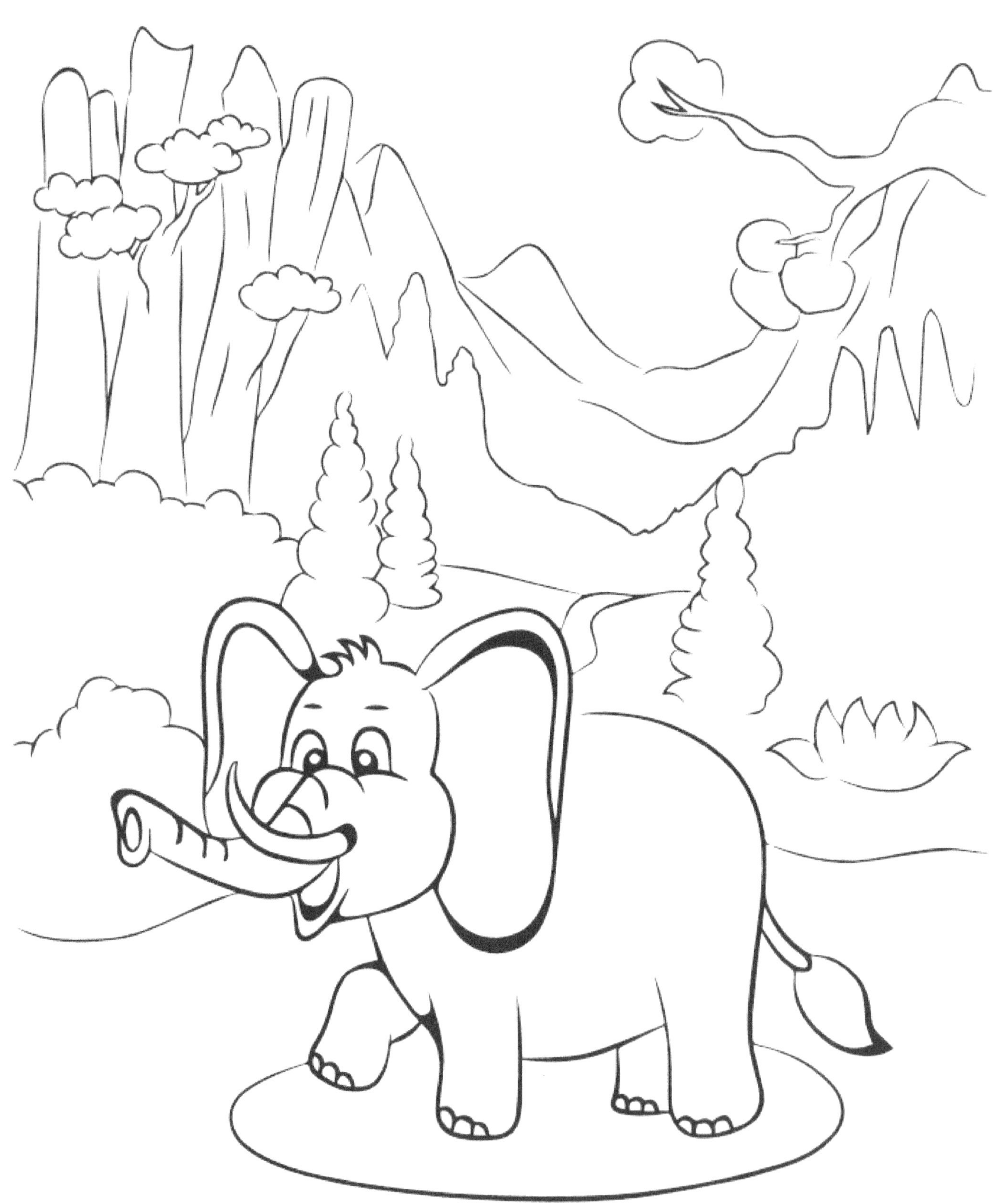

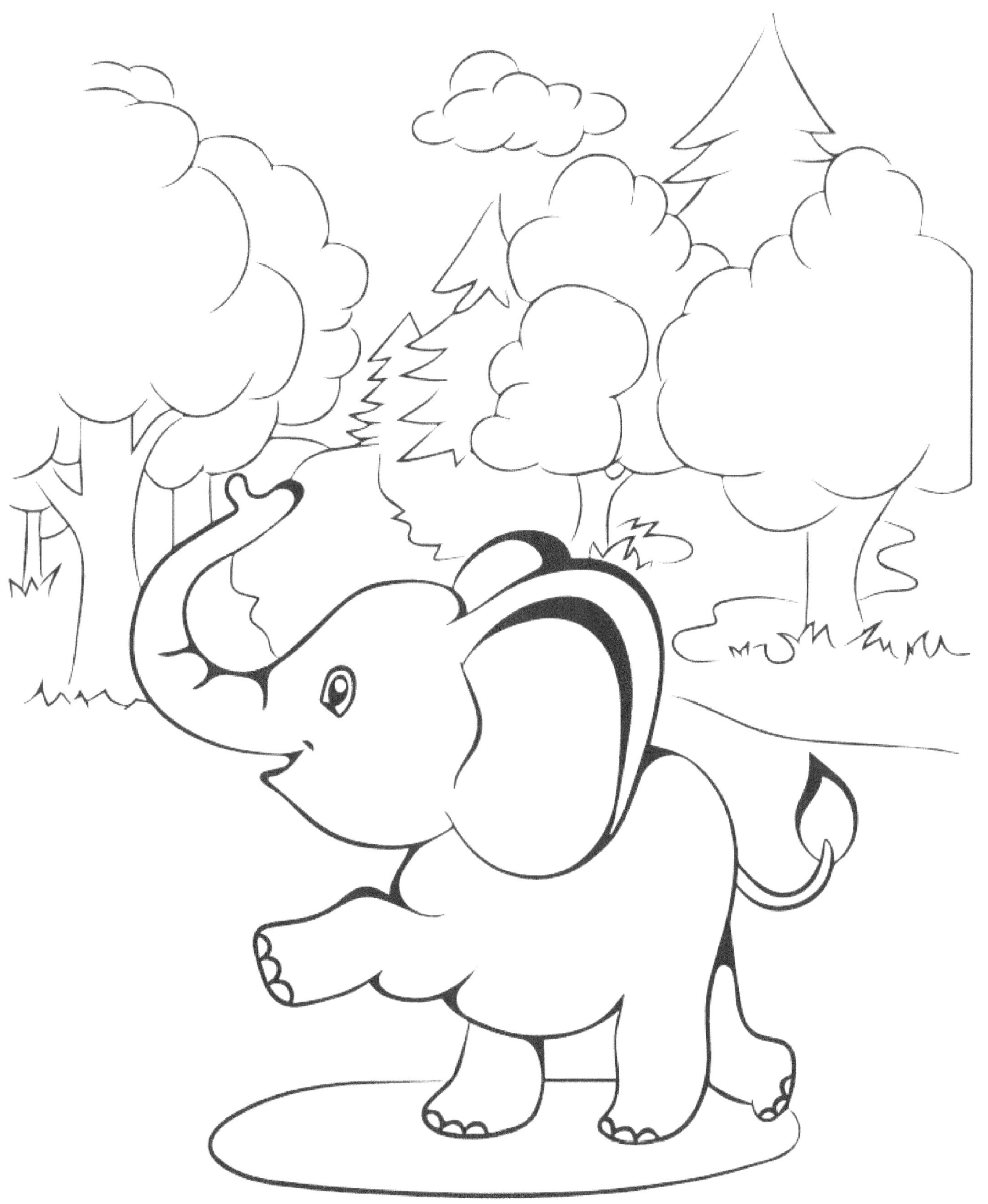

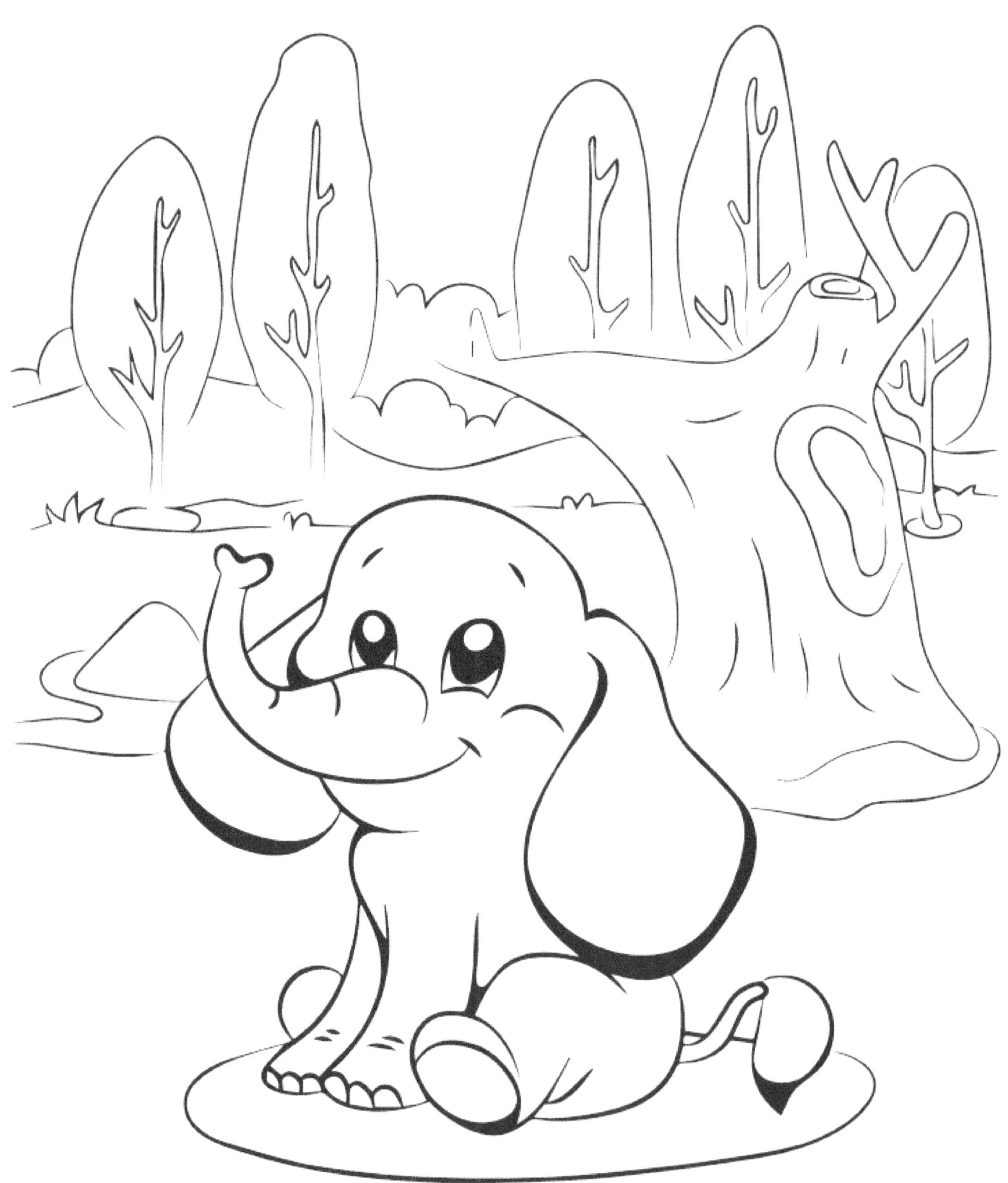

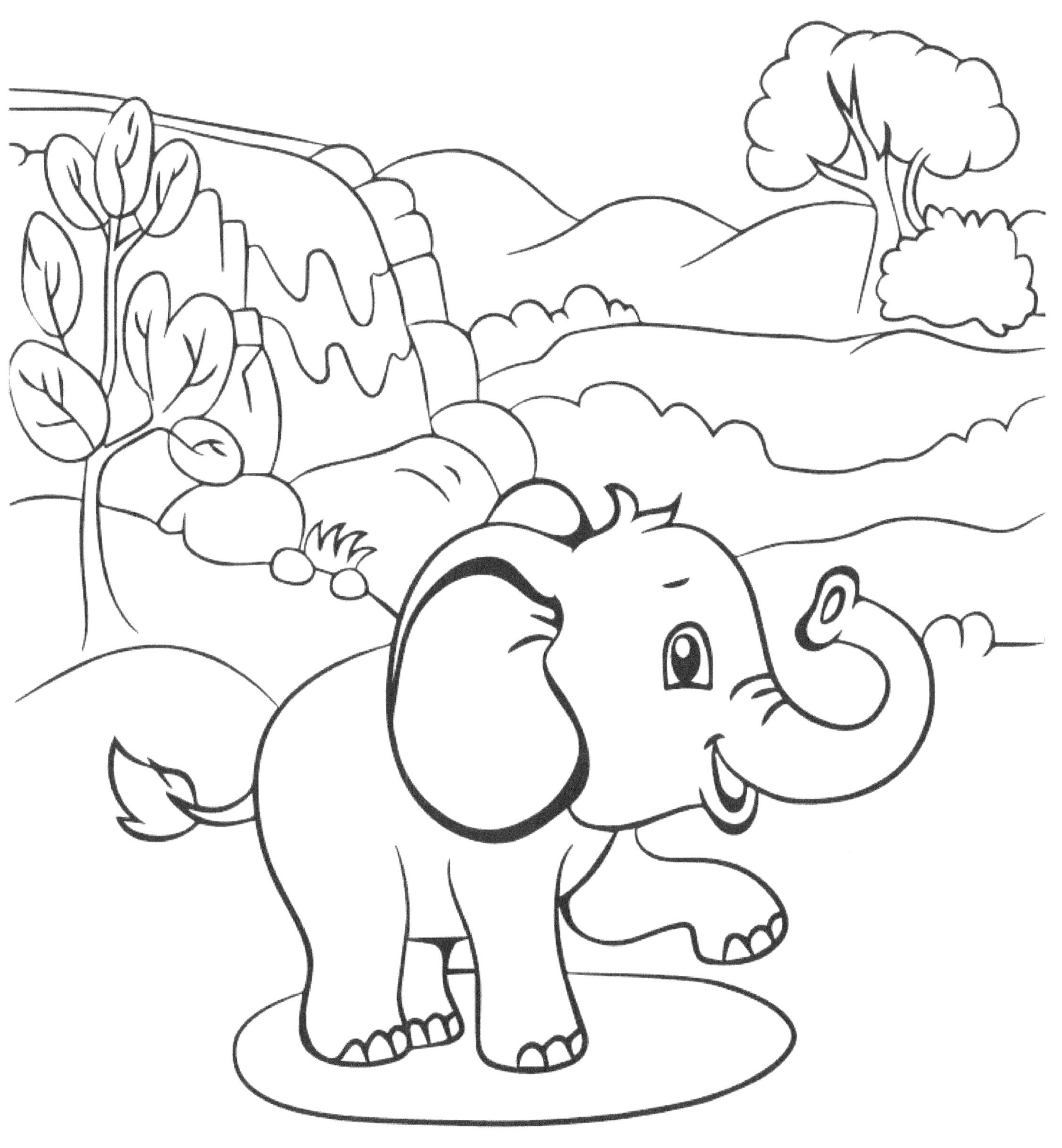

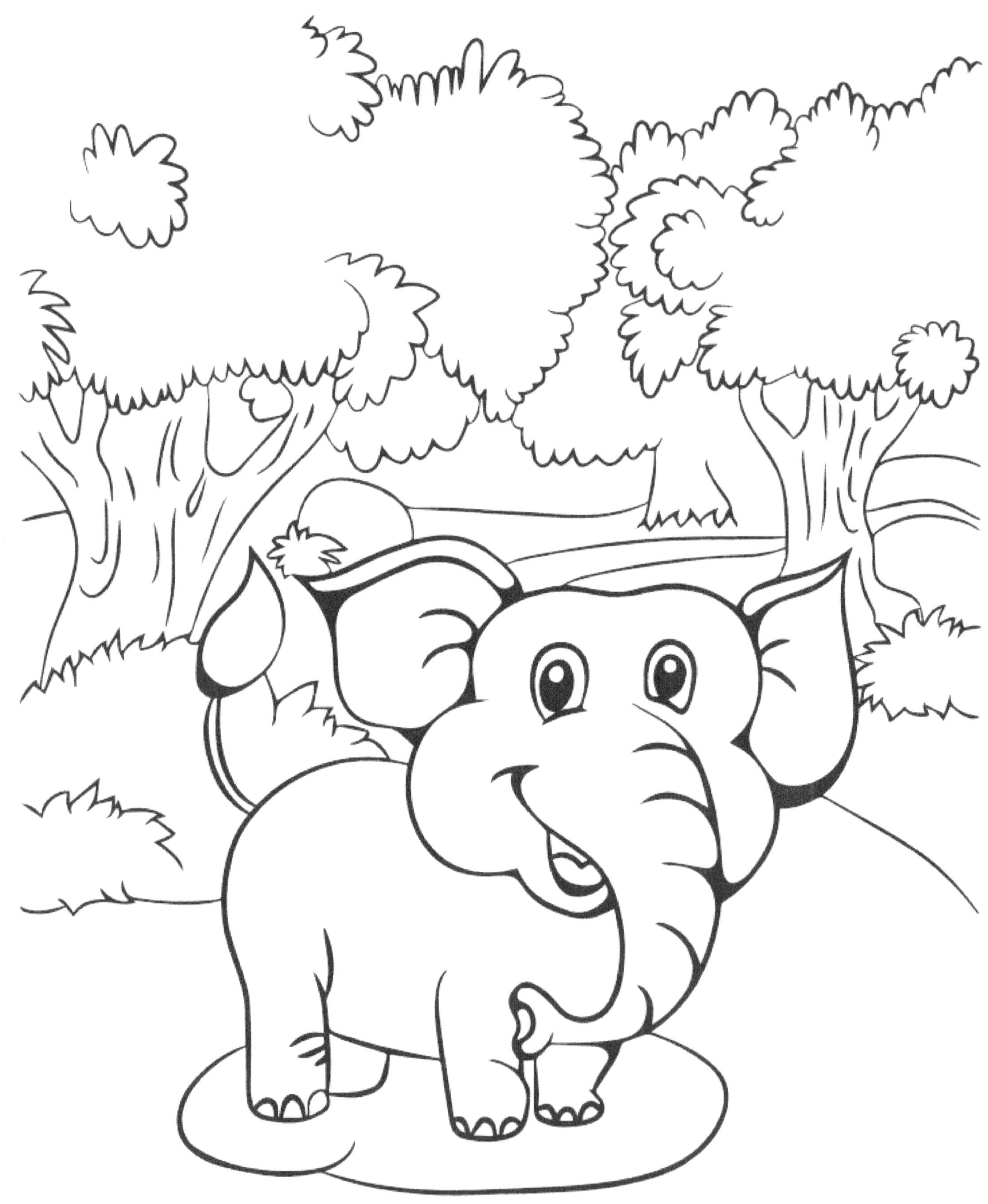

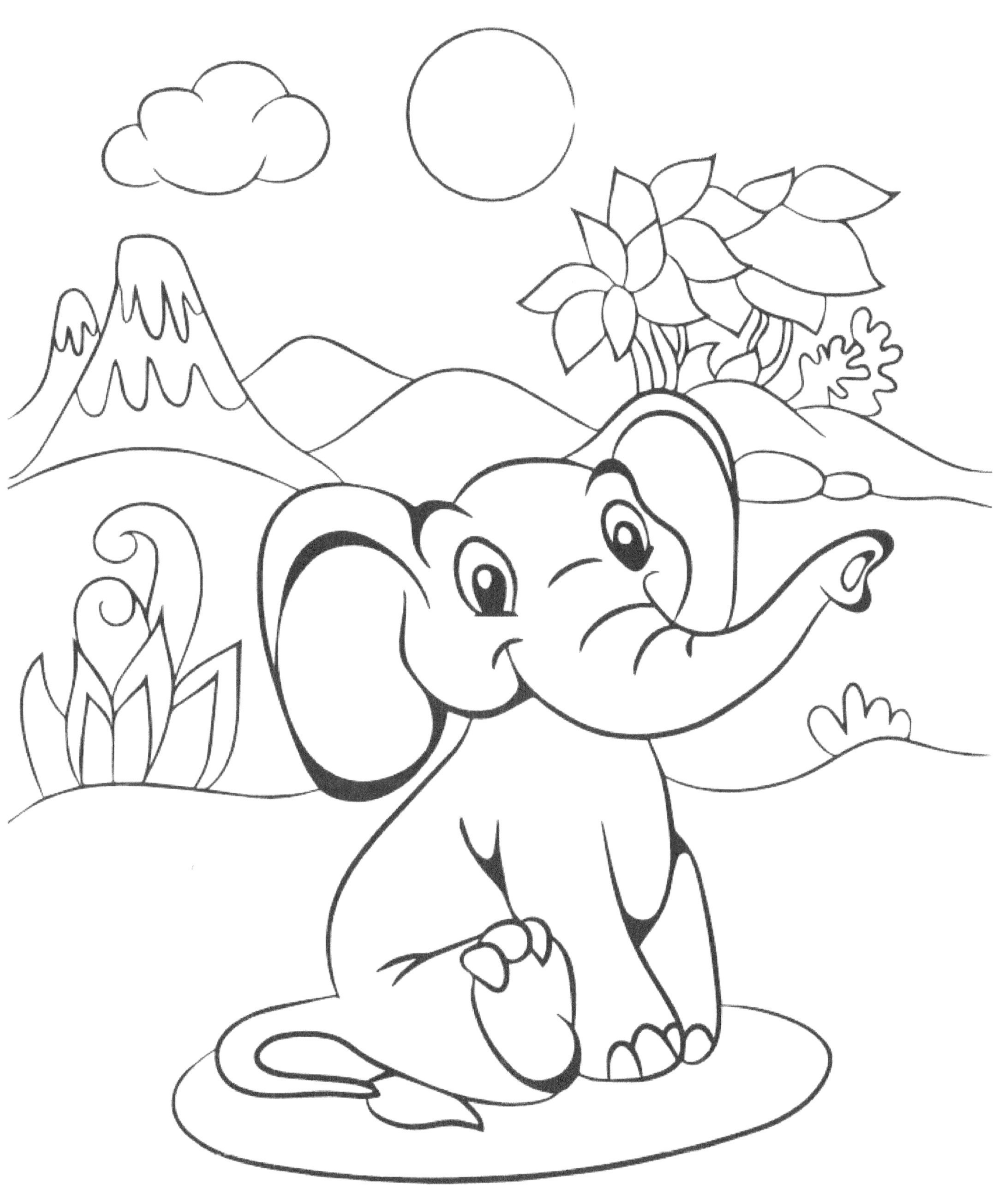

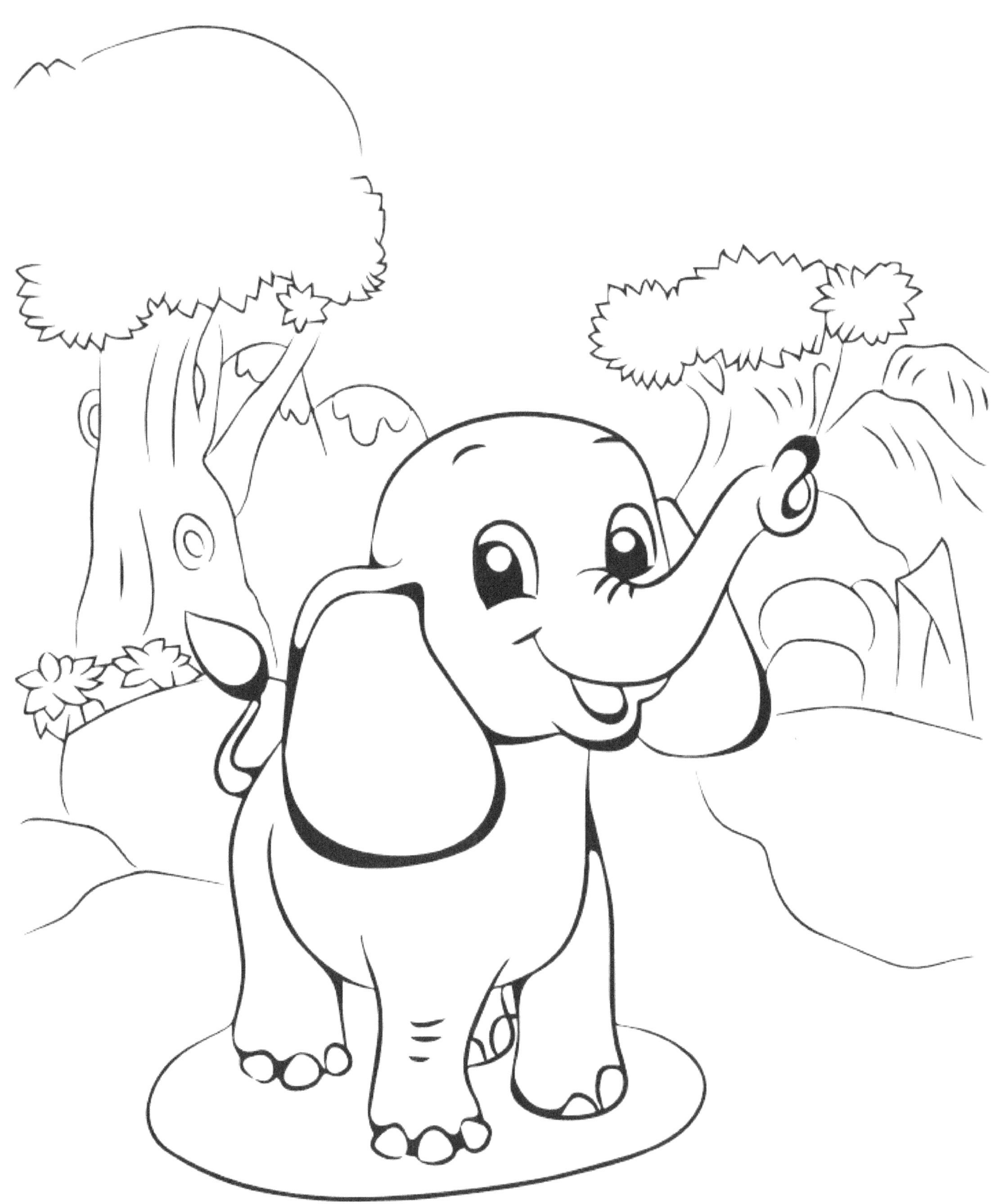

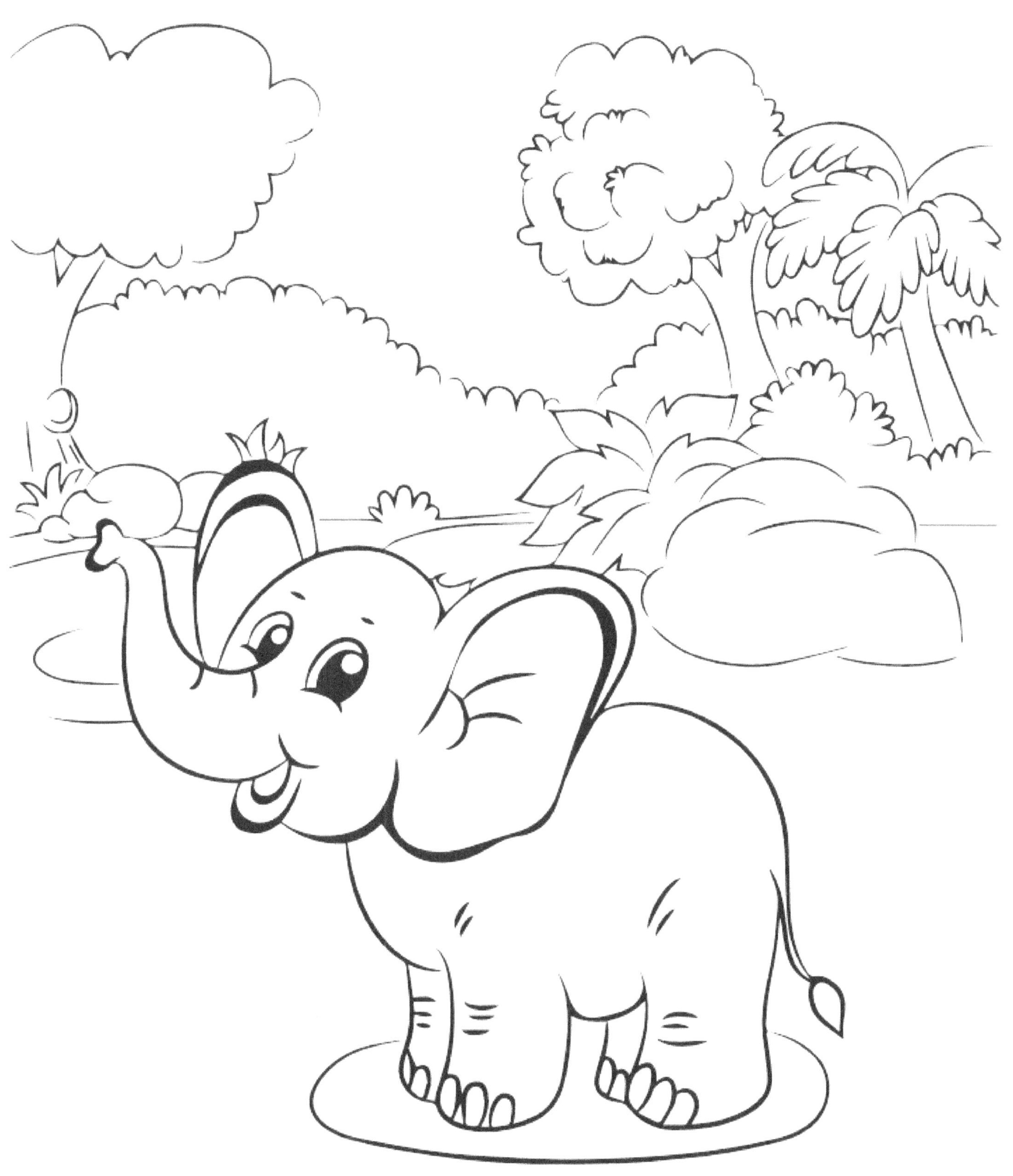

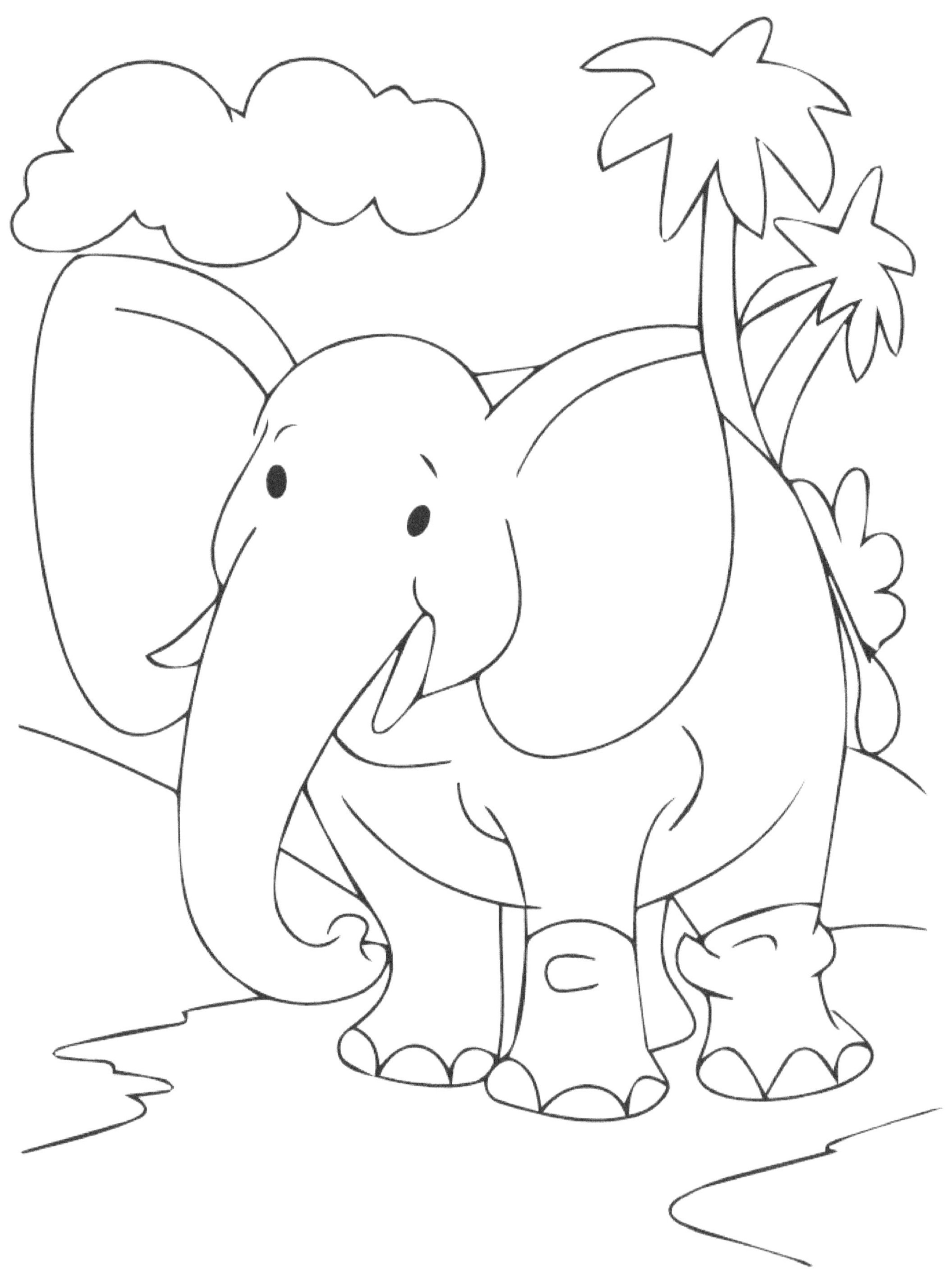

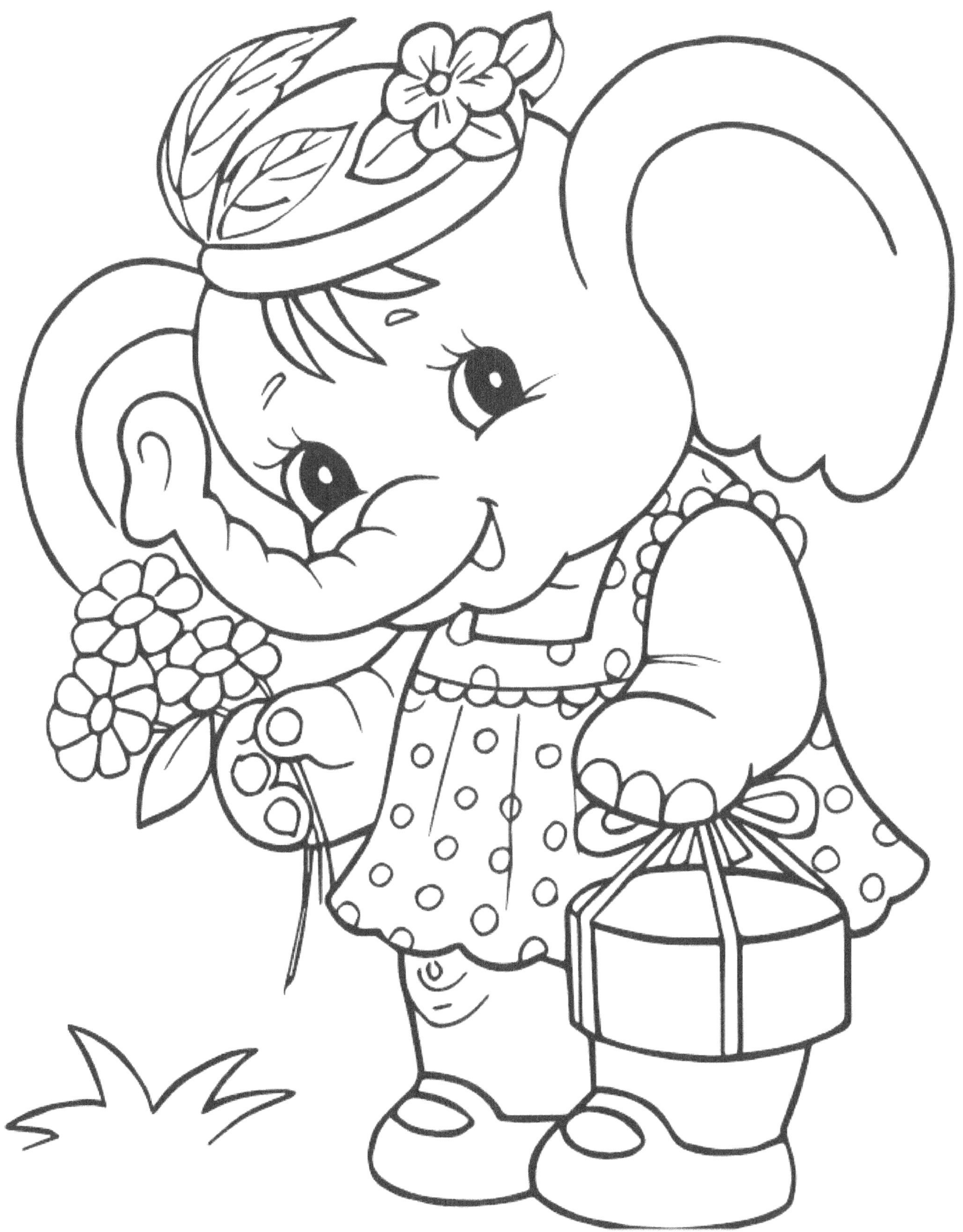

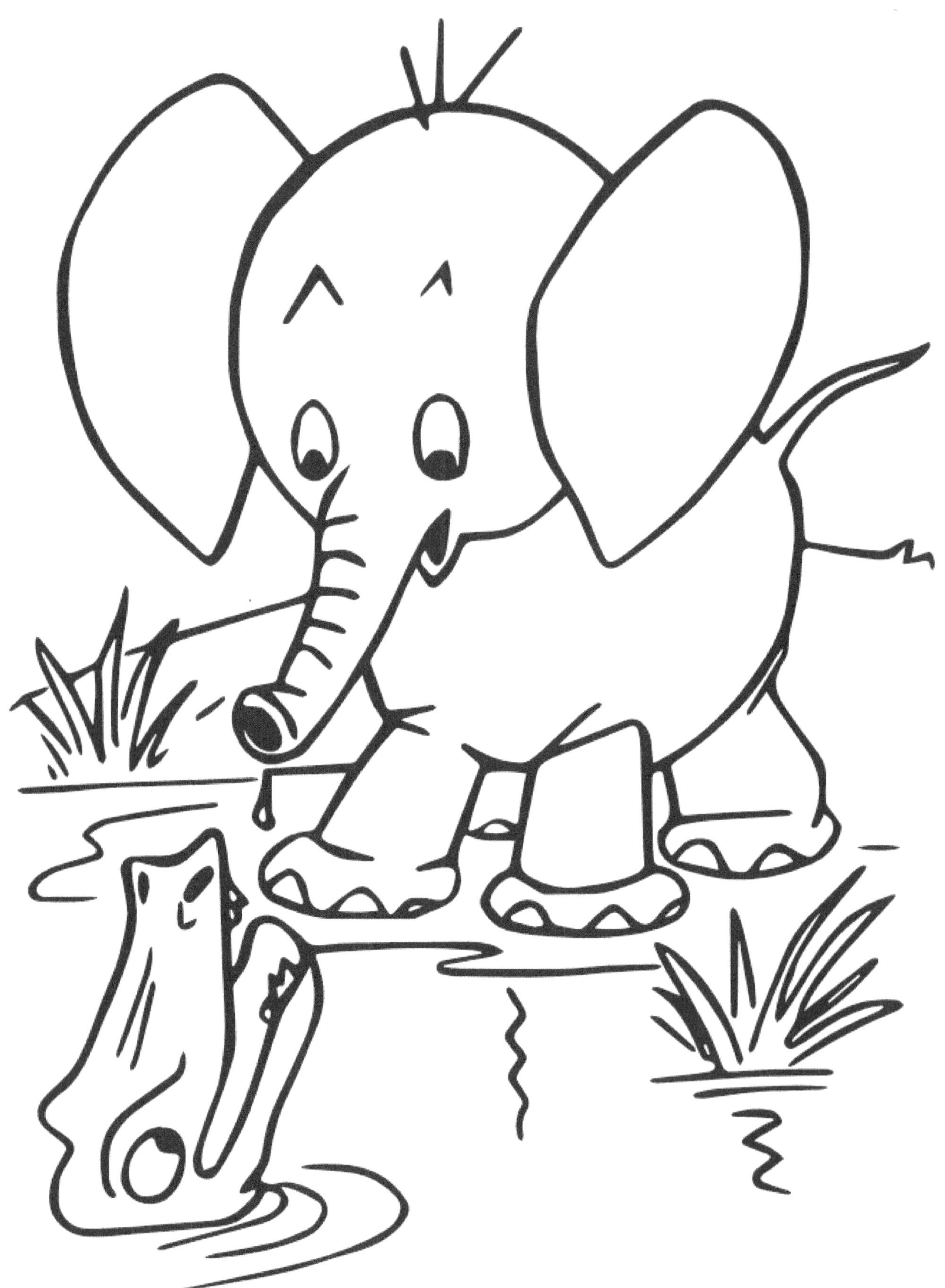

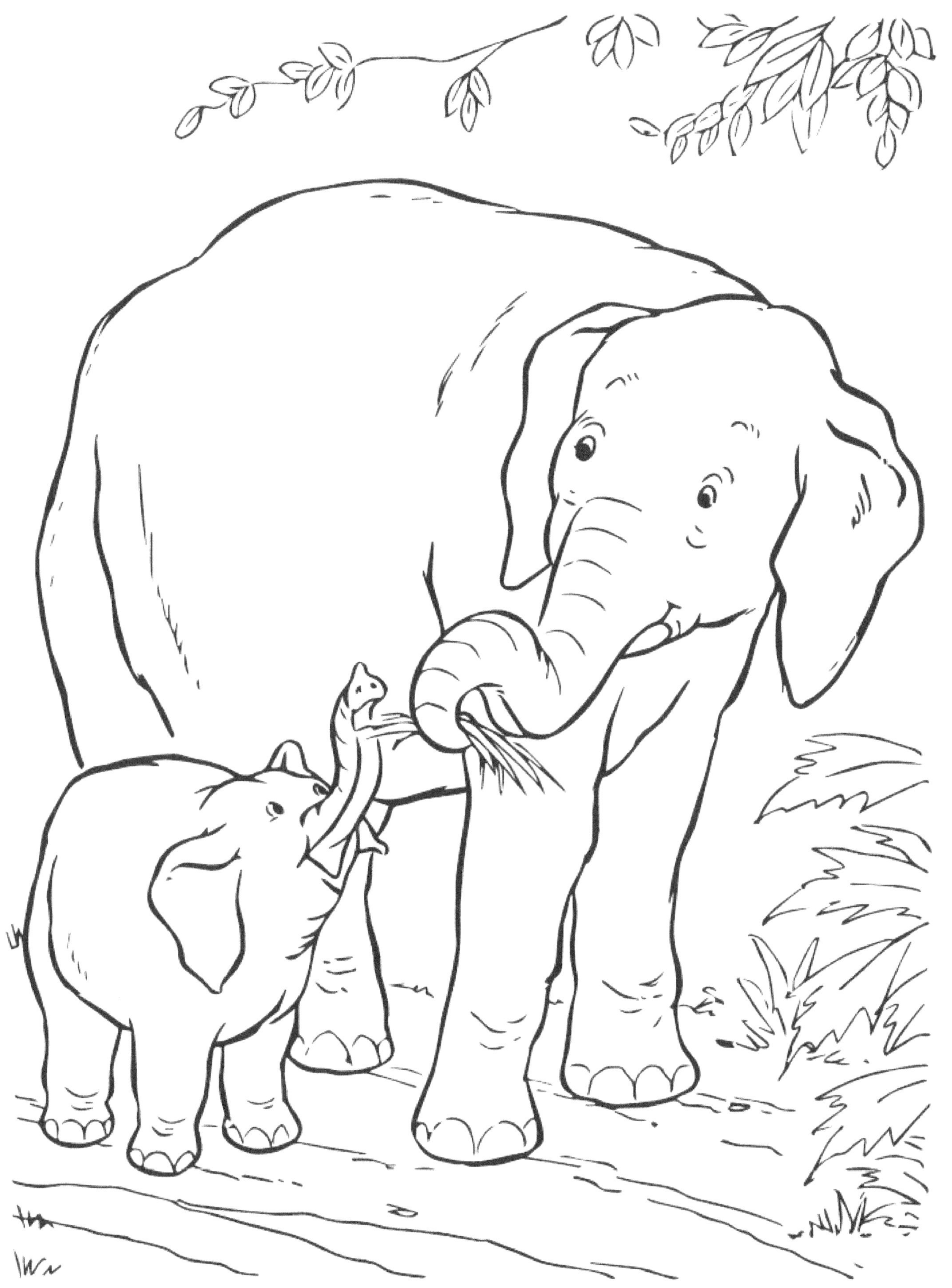

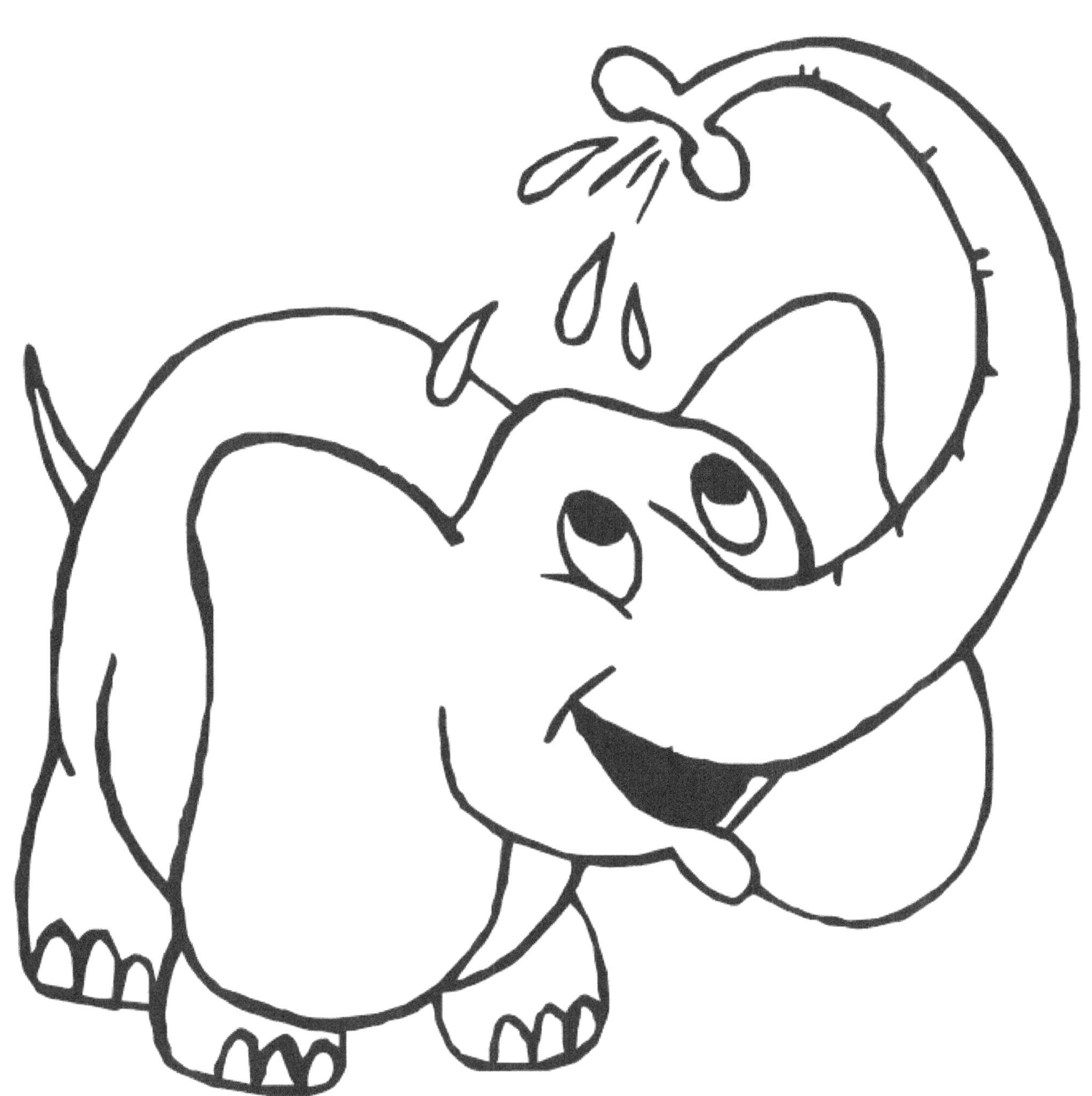

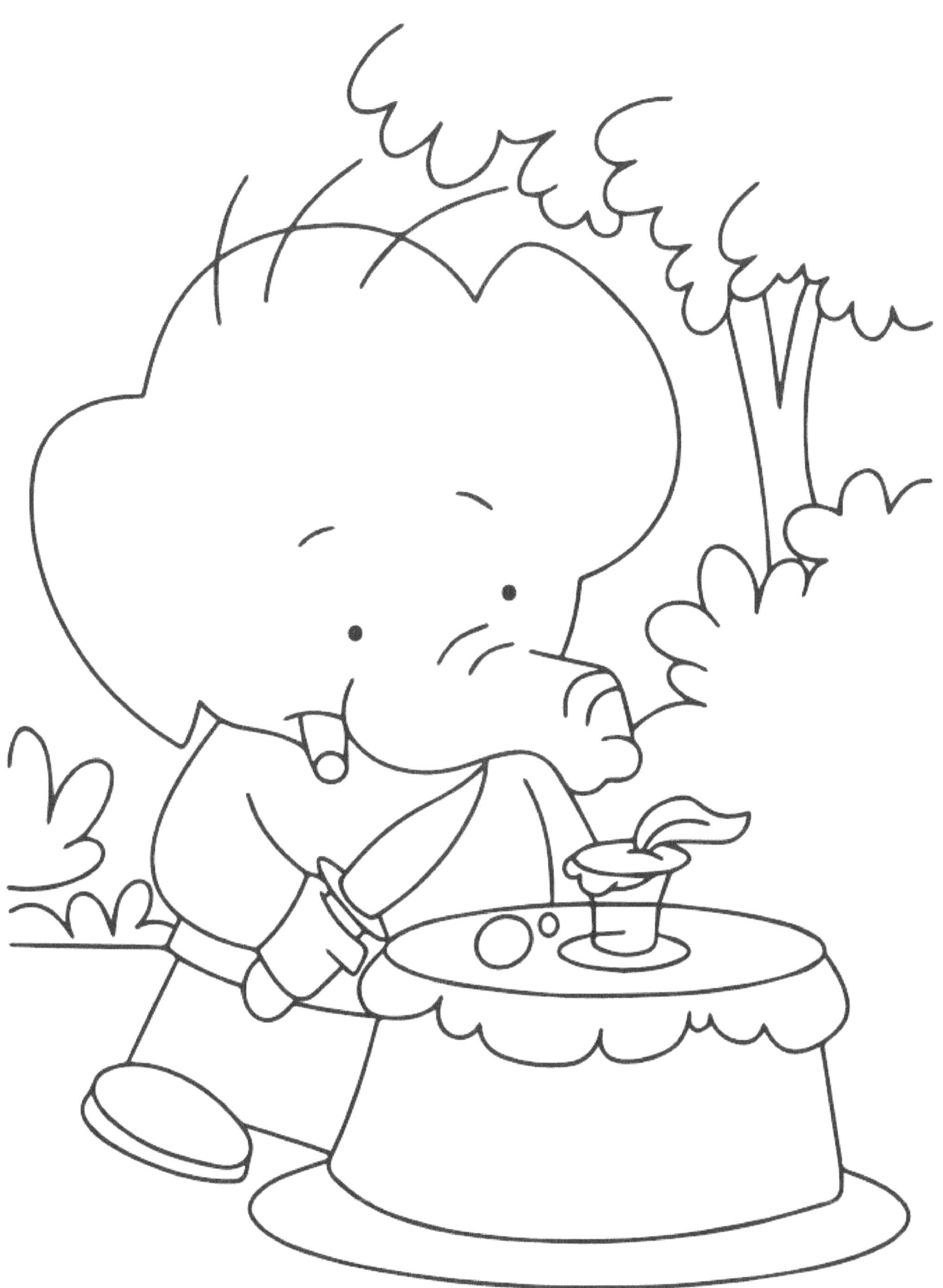

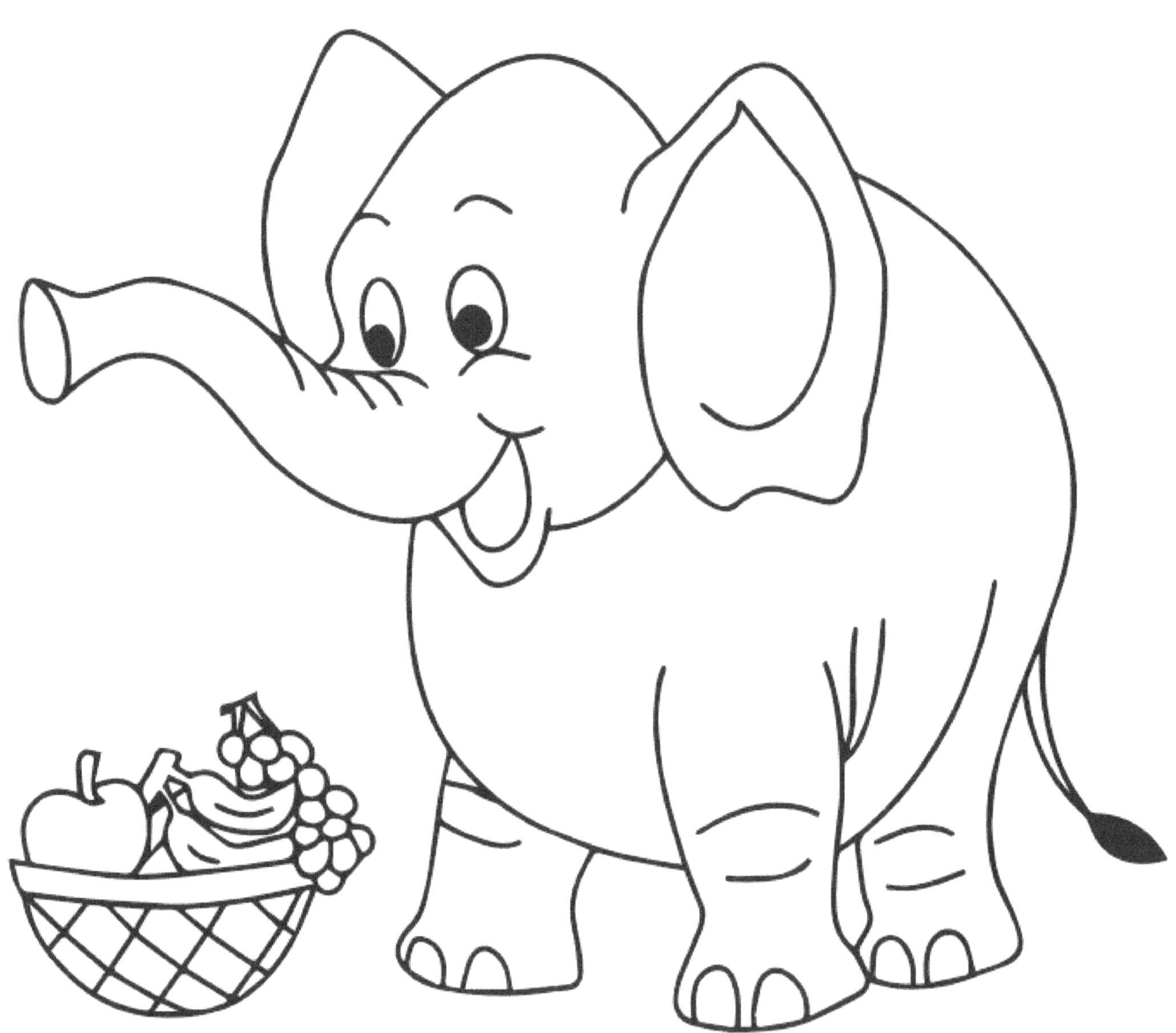

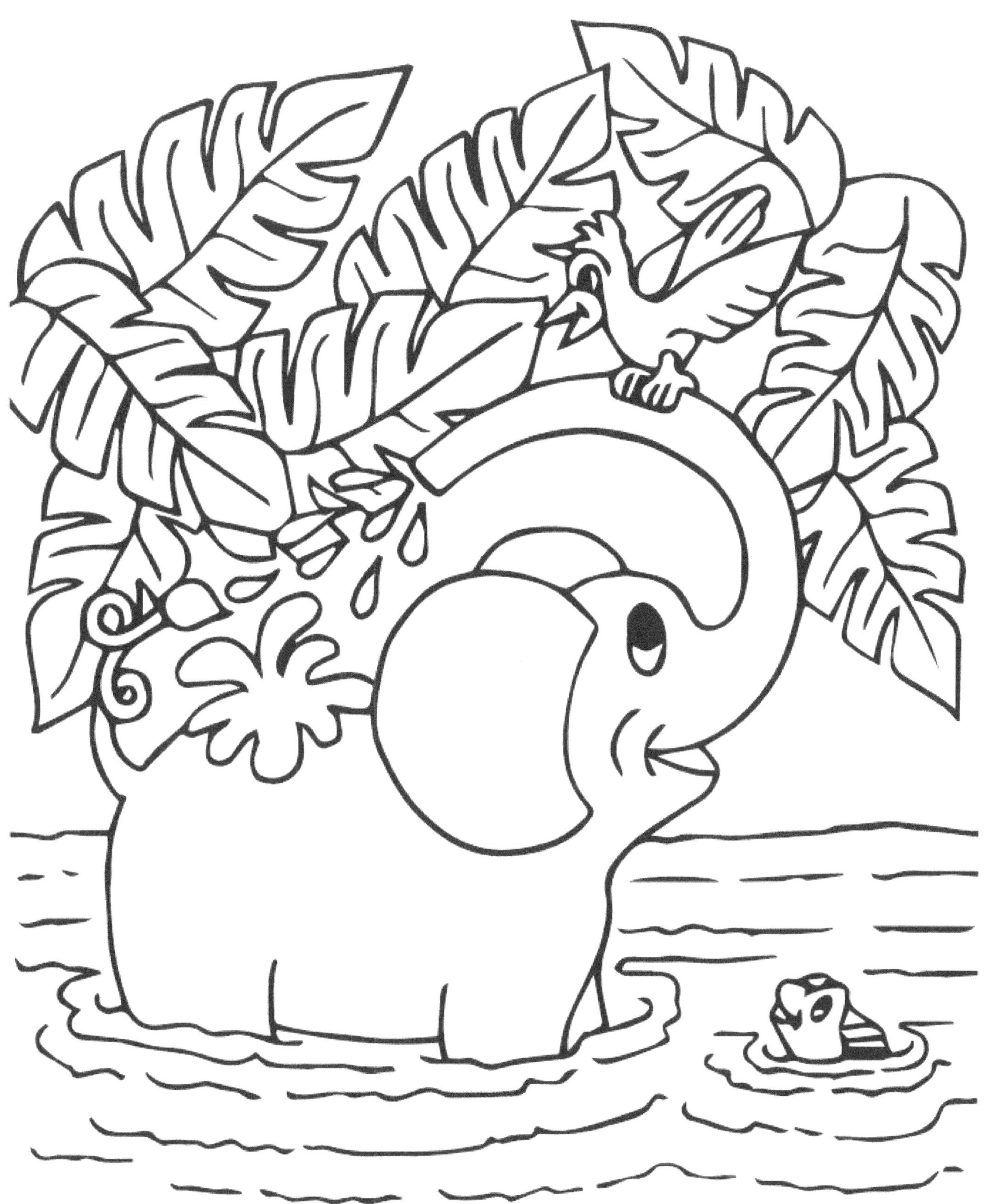

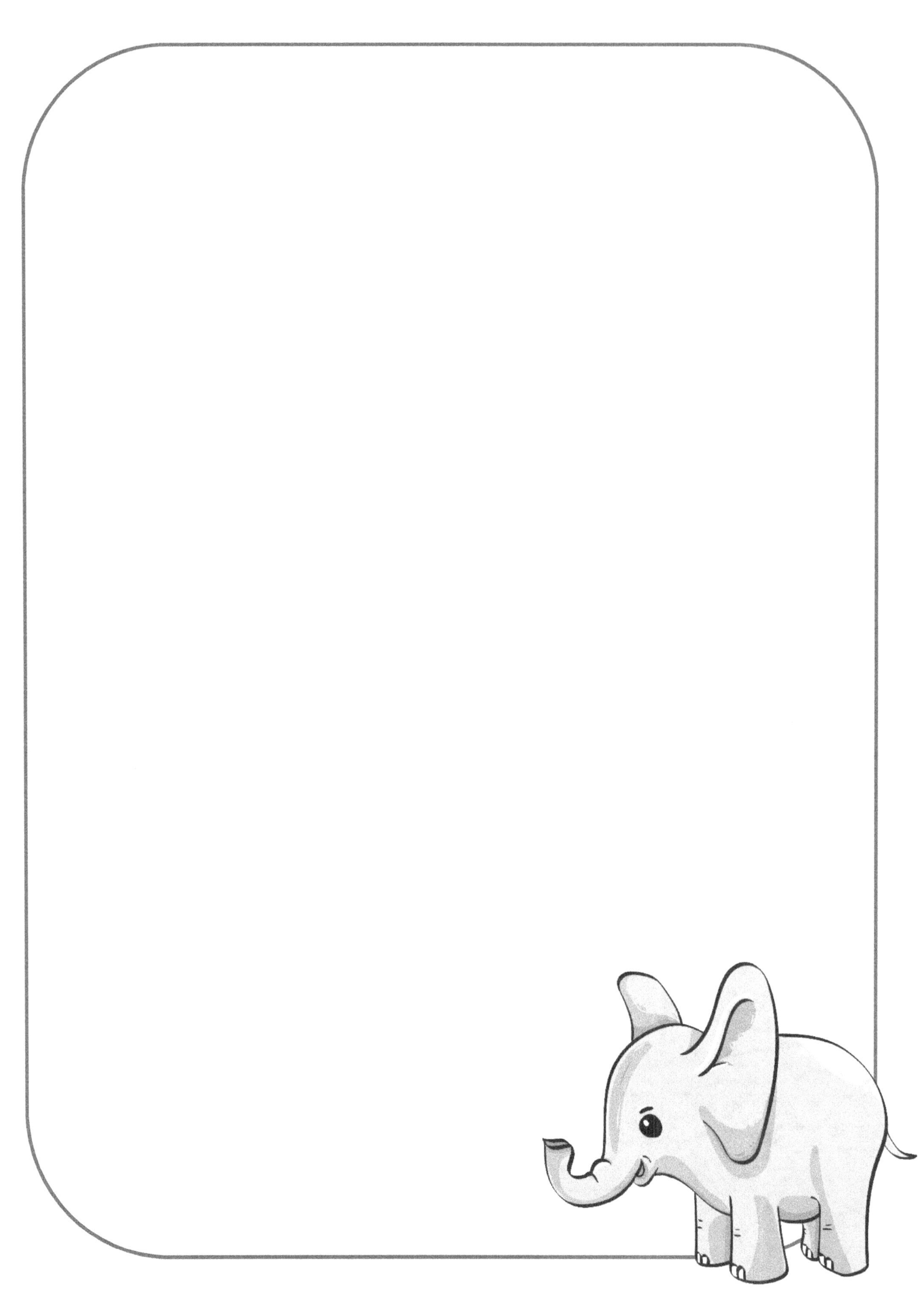

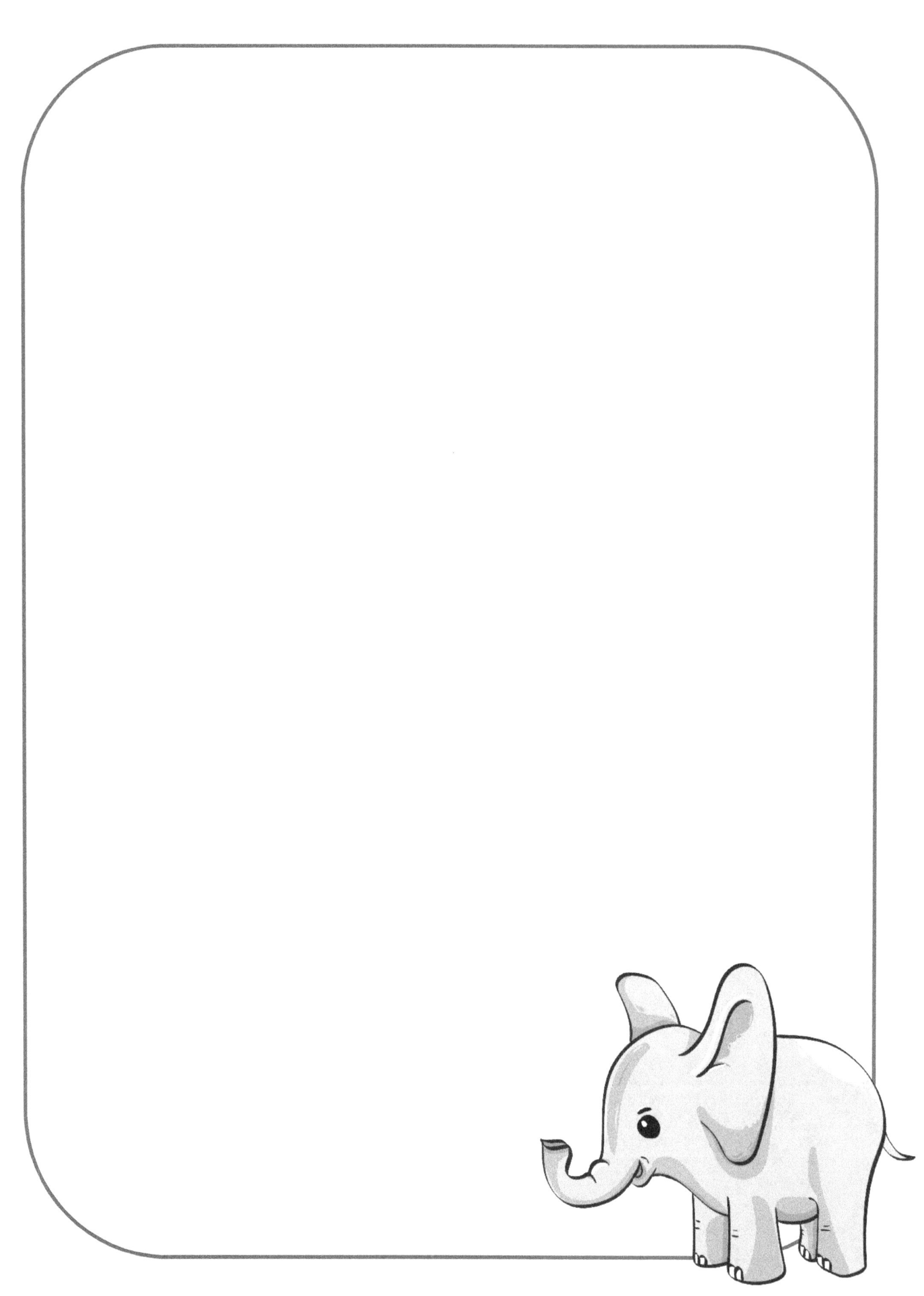